All about Squirrels and Moles and Things

By Althea

Illustrations by Christine Woodley
Graphics by Neil Grahame

Published for The National Trust
by Dinosaur Publications Limited

*ALL ABOUT SQUIRRELS AND MOLES
AND THINGS by Althea*

*This is the first book published for The National
Trust that is written specially for children.*

*People in the Trust like animals and try to help
them live happily in the woods and fields that
it owns.*

*If you want to see red squirrels, like the one on the
cover, one of the best places is Brownsea Island
in Poole Harbour. There are peacocks and herons
there, too.*

*We hope you enjoy reading this book, and
colouring the animals. Next time there may be
more books, perhaps about puffins or seals or
robins, so look out for them in the bookshops,
or when you next come to a place owned by the
National Trust.*

Squirrel

Red squirrels are quite rare now. Grey squirrels have chased them away from their homes.

Red squirrels have a reddish-brown fur coat with white markings on the chest. High up in the trees, they build nests out of twigs which they line with moss. They run up and down the trunks, and leap through the air from one tree to another with their bushy tails flying out behind them. Sometimes they play hide and seek with each other in the trees. They can hang onto a branch with just their back feet if they want to reach out to pick some tasty buds or leaves.

Squirrels eat nuts and acorns. They use their paws like hands, and sit up on their haunches to nibble their food. They can easily cut through the shell of a nut with their sharp teeth. In the autumn they store food away by digging holes in the ground so that they have something to eat during the winter.

Squirrels have their families in the spring, usually in April. They have three or four babies.

Mole

Moles have soft velvety fur which is almost black. They have a snout rather like a pig, and very small eyes. They cannot see very well. Their ears and eyes are well hidden by their fur so the soil does not get in them when they are digging.

Moles spend most of their time under the ground in tunnels which they dig with their big front paws. You can sometimes see piles of earth which they have pushed up, when making their tunnels. These bumps of earth are called mole hills. Moles make nests underground with grass and leaves which they carry down in their mouths. They usually have lots of ways in and out so that they can escape from one hole if anything tries to get in through another.

Moles usually have about five babies in the springtime. Moles eat worms and slugs and snails and other insects. They drink a lot and can swim quite well too.

Dormouse

A dormouse is very small and he is a gingery colour with big black eyes. Dormice live in all sorts of places, but mostly in hedges and bushes where they make a round nest woven out of straw and grass. They eat nuts and fruit and they also like beetles and other insects.

They are very sleepy animals, and only wake up at night. In the winter they curl up in their nests, wrap their tails over their faces, and sleep so soundly that they do not awake even if picked up!

In the spring the baby mice are born. There are usually about three and they are very small indeed. But soon they begin to grow, and to run about squeaking and washing their faces and grooming their whiskers with their front paws.

Hedgehog

Hedgehogs are brown and yellowy coloured and they are covered in prickles which usually lie flat. But if they are worried, by a dog for instance, they roll up into a ball and make their prickles stand out so that people can't bother them. They can also roll up in a ball to go down hills. Baby hedgehogs have to learn to do this and it takes them several weeks to be taught how by their mothers.

Hedgehogs live on insects, but sometimes they eat birds' eggs. They live in nests made mainly of grass and twigs in the hedges. Hedgehogs usually have two families a year, one in late spring, and the other about September. They have several babies at a time and the mother hedgehog feeds them with her milk and the babies keep squeaking for more.

Their main enemy is the fox, who tries to catch them and eat them. They sleep all winter, only coming out on odd days when the sun is shining to get some food and hurry back with it to their nests.

Badger

Badgers have white faces with a broad black stripe on each side. The rest of their fur looks grey but is really made up of black and white hairs. The underneath of their body is black. As they usually go out at night, they are very difficult to see except for their faces, which are supposed to look frightening to their enemies.

They live in holes called sets, which they dig out of the ground. You can sometimes find their sets, because they always use a tree near the entrance to sharpen their claws and you can see the scratches. They build so many passages and rooms that rabbits and foxes sometimes move in with them! They usually let the rabbits stay but chase away the foxes. Badgers are very clean animals and change their bedding two or three times a year. They collect a bundle of bracken and leaves, and holding it against their front legs with their heads, they shuffle backwards into their sets.

They eat slugs, worms, and beetles, and grass and roots too. They search out and destroy wasps nests, and eat up the grubs.

They have two or three babies in February or March, and the young badgers stay with their parents until September, before going out into the world on their own.

Bat

Bats are rather strange animals, and apart from birds and insects, they are the only creatures that fly using wings. They have a very small mouse-like body. Their wings are attached to their front legs.

They are very difficult to find because they sleep during the daytime. At twilight they come out and start flying around looking for insects for food. They can fly very fast in the dark without bumping into things. They do this by making very high-pitched squeaks as they fly and hearing how close they are to things by how quickly the squeak comes back to them. This gives them a sound picture rather like we get a sight picture with our eyes. They shut their ears so that they don't deafen themselves when they squeak, and open them in time to hear the sound echoing back.

Bats hibernate in the winter and go into a very deep sleep until the weather gets warmer in the spring.

Rabbit

There are lots of wild rabbits in this country. They are usually brown. You can sometimes see them playing in the fields. They mostly eat grass and plants such as dandelion leaves, and they love to nibble carrots, and young shoots, and can do a lot of damage to crops.

They live in underground holes called burrows, which they dig out of the earth. They make lots of passages, and have many ways of getting in and out.

The female rabbit is called a doe, and the male a buck. Rabbits have six or seven big families every year, sometimes seven or eight babies to look after at a time.

Rabbits have long ears and can hear very well. If you surprise one it may crouch down absolutely still hoping it won't be noticed. Then it will dash away faster than you can run, with its white tail bobbing up and down, until it disappears down one of the entrances to its burrow.

Deer

There are lots of different kinds of deer in Britain. Some of them originally came from other countries but now live here all the time. A male deer is called a buck or stag, and a female one a doe. Most male deer have horns and these sometimes grow into fine antlers with lots of branches, almost like a tree. Deer eat grass and other plants and they like acorns and berries too. Sometimes they damage small branches of trees by eating the bark. They usually rest during the daytime and in the evening they can be seen coming out to feed. They usually move about at night, perhaps because they feel safer.

When stags are choosing wives, which they do once a year, they sometimes have arguments between themselves and fight with their antlers. Deer often move about in groups called herds. In the spring, the does go to a quiet place and have their young calves. Usually there is only one baby, but sometimes there are twins. Within a few hours, the young calves can walk about and even run a little, but for months they cannot feed themselves and live on their mother's milk.

Stoat

Stoats belong to the weasel family. They are long and slim and perky-looking and they have long whiskers. They live in tiny caves or holes in the ground. When the time for having babies comes in late April, they make a nest from dry leaves and grass and the family of three or four is born. The mother stoat feeds them with her milk and also brings them dead mice and other small animals to eat.

When they change their coats in the wintertime, their fur sometimes turns white which makes it easy for them to hide in the snow when they are hunting. They are very good hunters and they can easily kill a rat.

Stoats, or ermine, belong to the same family as weasels, badgers and otters.

Fox

Strangely enough, foxes are cousins to dogs. They are reddish-brown in colour, the backs of their ears are black, and they have white markings underneath their bodies and on their throats. The fox hunts mainly at night, hiding during the day in holes or burrows which are called earths. Sometimes they move into rabbits' and badgers' holes.

It is not often you hear foxes, but sometimes on a winter night you can hear the female fox, which is called a vixen, making a yapping scream, or the male barking like a dog. Foxes mostly hunt hares, rabbits and game birds. In wintertime they are brave enough to attack poultry yards quite near to houses, and have been known to carry off young lambs, too.

Foxes are very intelligent and they will jump up onto trees, swim across streams or hide amongst sheep in order to escape being caught. Farmers consider them a pest and they are often hunted by hounds and men on horseback.